FIRST NAME: MARGUERITE
LAST NAME: HANNAN
DATE OF BIRTH: Nov 6, 1974
TEST DATE: FEB 21, 2023
TEST TIME: 10:00 PM

FIRST NAME: MOLLY
LAST NAME: HANNAN
DATE OF BIRTH: JAN 15, 1944
TEST DATE: FEB 21, 2023
TEST TIME: 10:00 PM

Made in the USA
Las Vegas, NV
07 October 2021